I0473140

ZHINGOORA BOOKS

MATHEW CLIFF

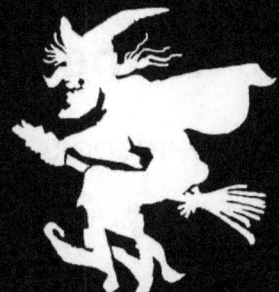

A
WITCH
STENCILS
BOOK

A

Witch Stencils Book

BY

Mathew cliff

[ZHINGOORA BOOKS]

This paperback edition is published by Zhingoora Books.

The Cover is Designed by Pallav Sethiya.

Apart from any fair dealing for the purposes of research or private study, or criti-cism or review, this publication may only be reproduced, stored or transmitted, in any form or by any means, with the prior permission in writing of the publishers. All disputes are subject to exclusive jurisdiction of Mandsaur Courts only. For any suggestions and feedback or book on new concept/domain, please contact us at the email given below.
zhingoora_books@yahoo.com

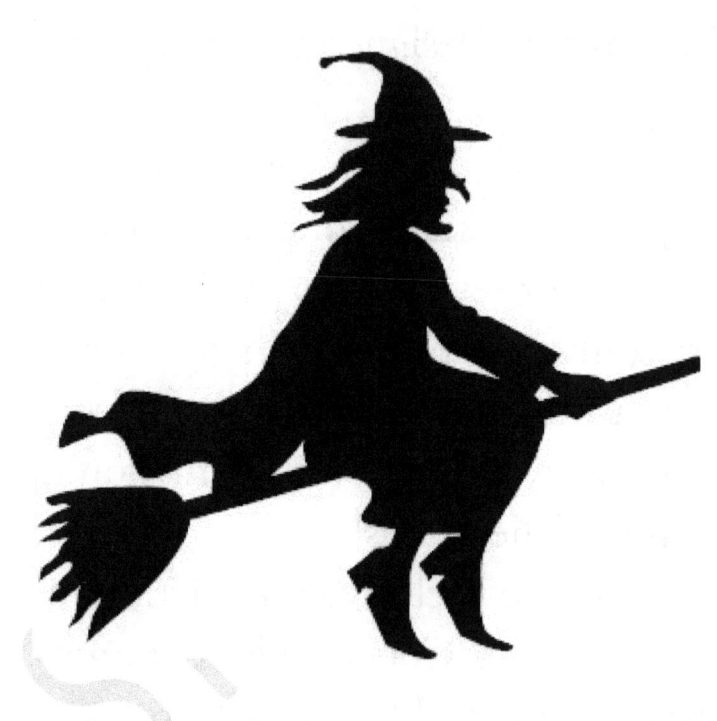

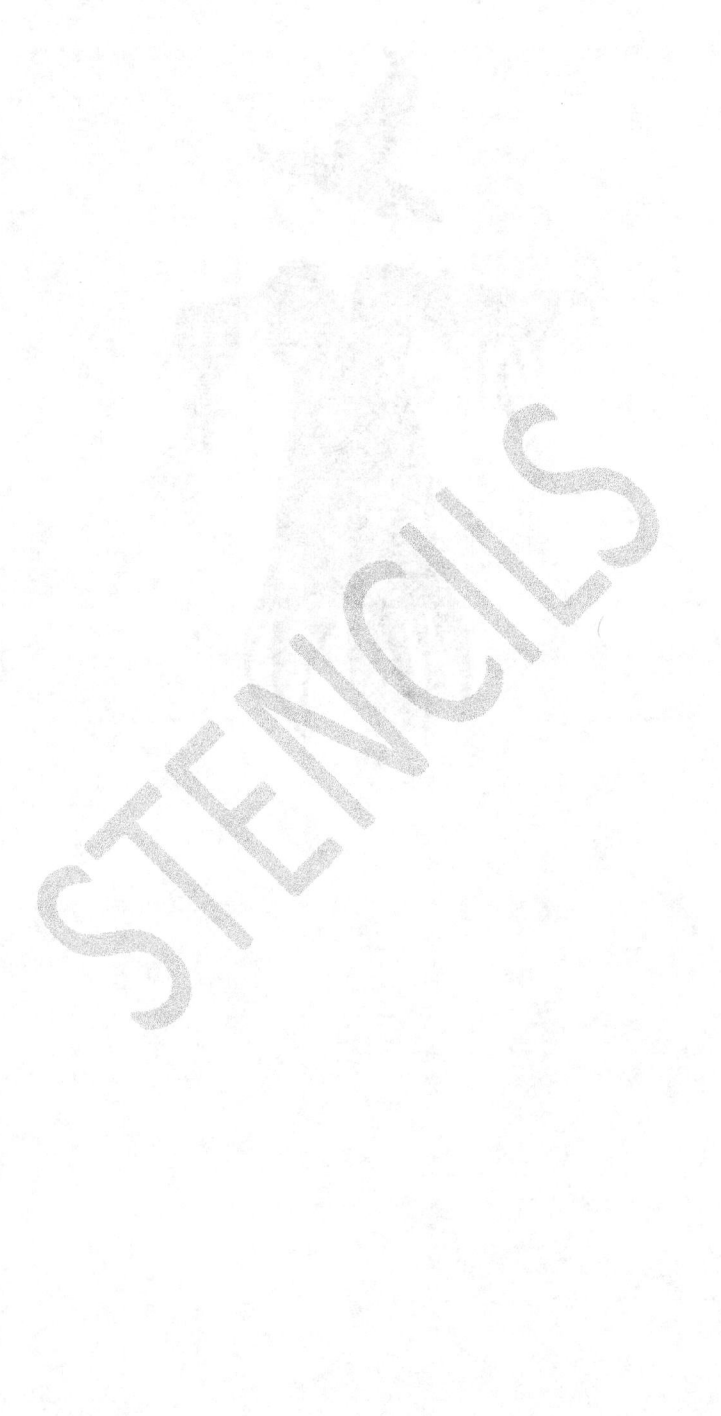

STENCILS

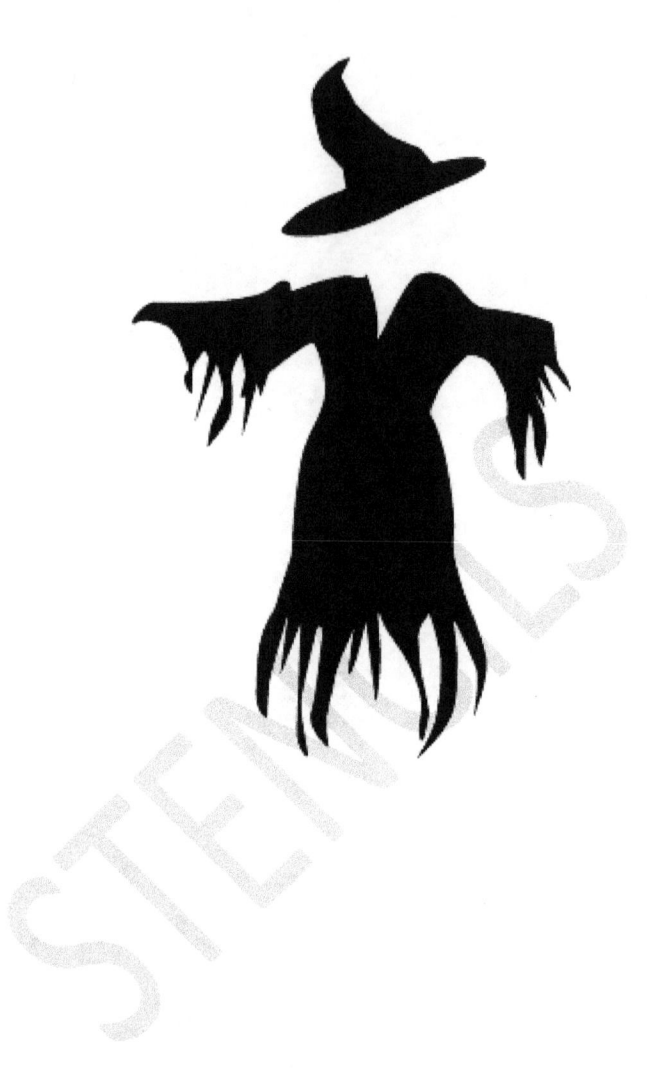
STENCILS

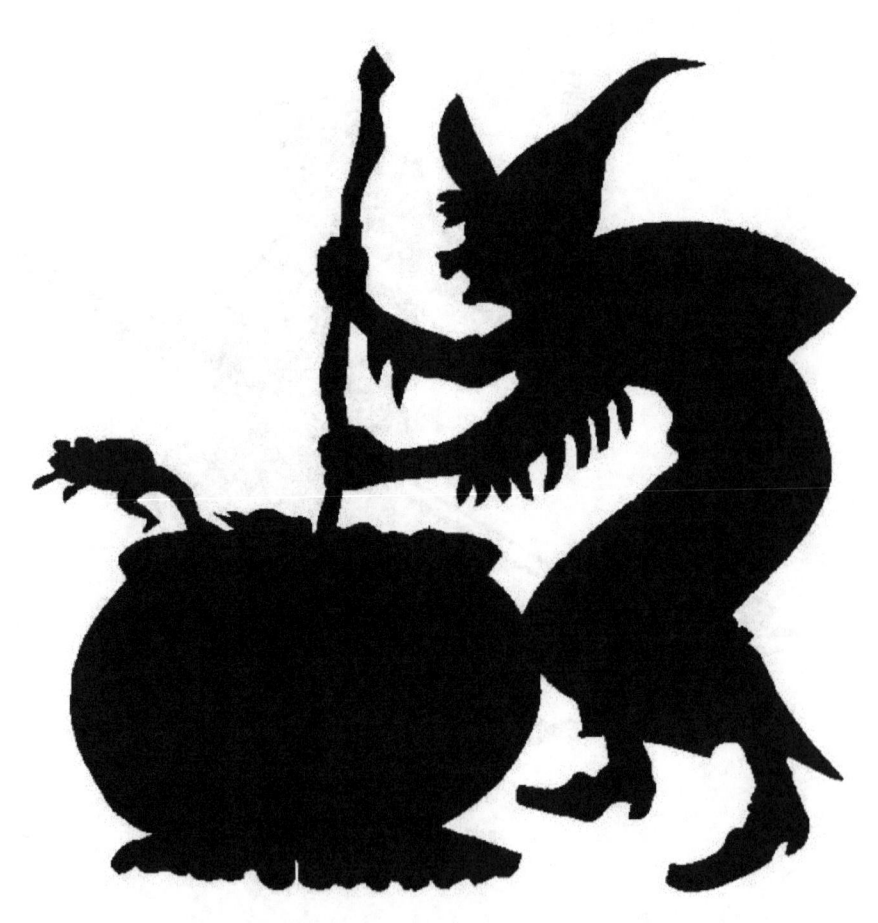

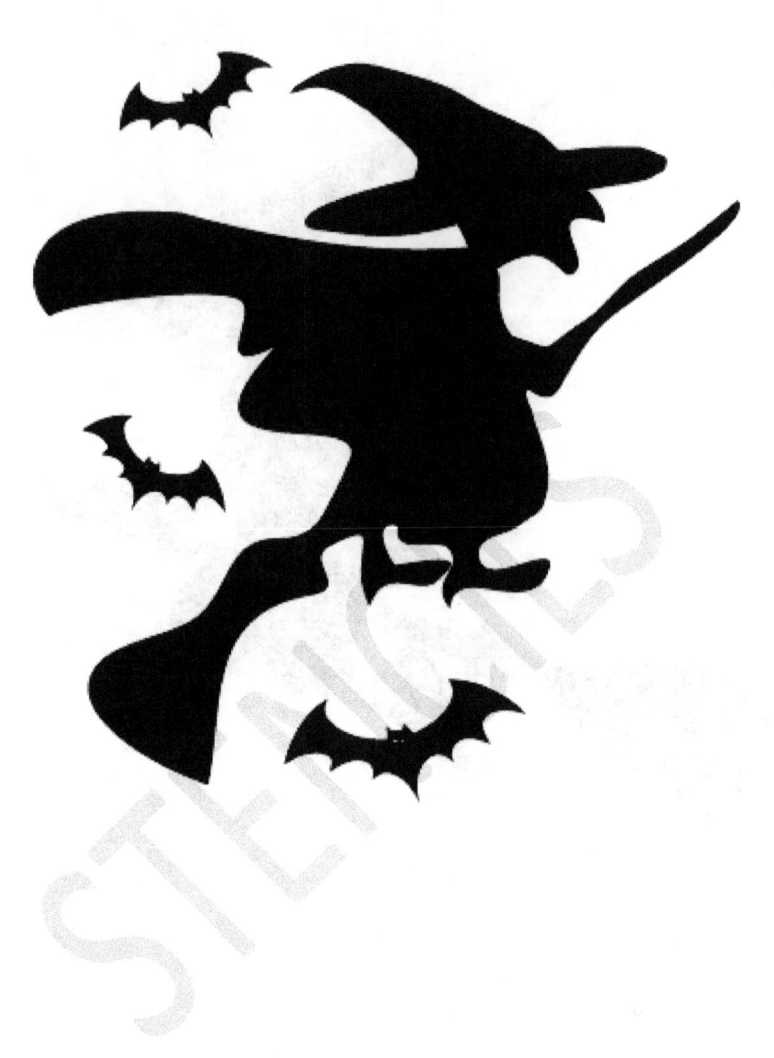

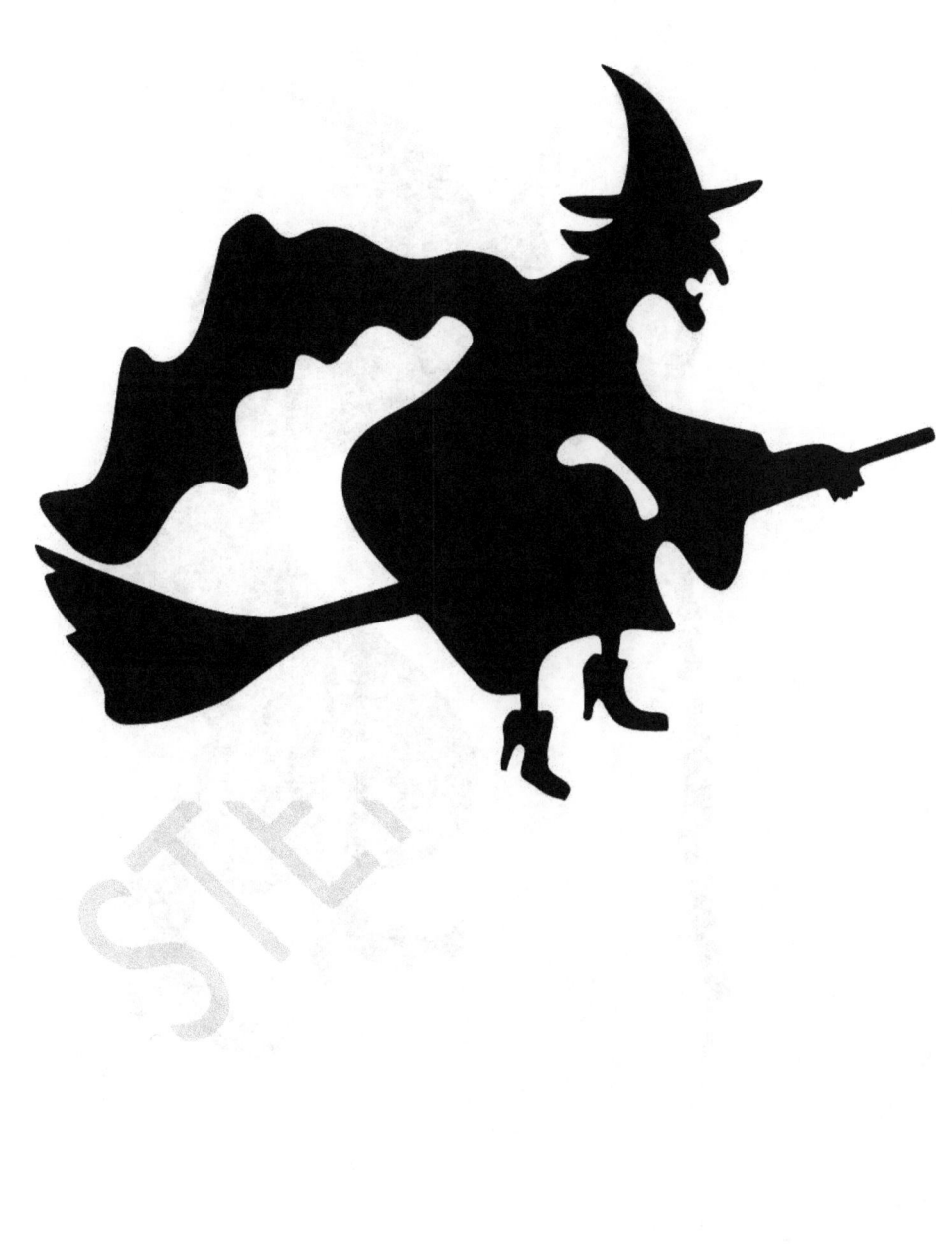

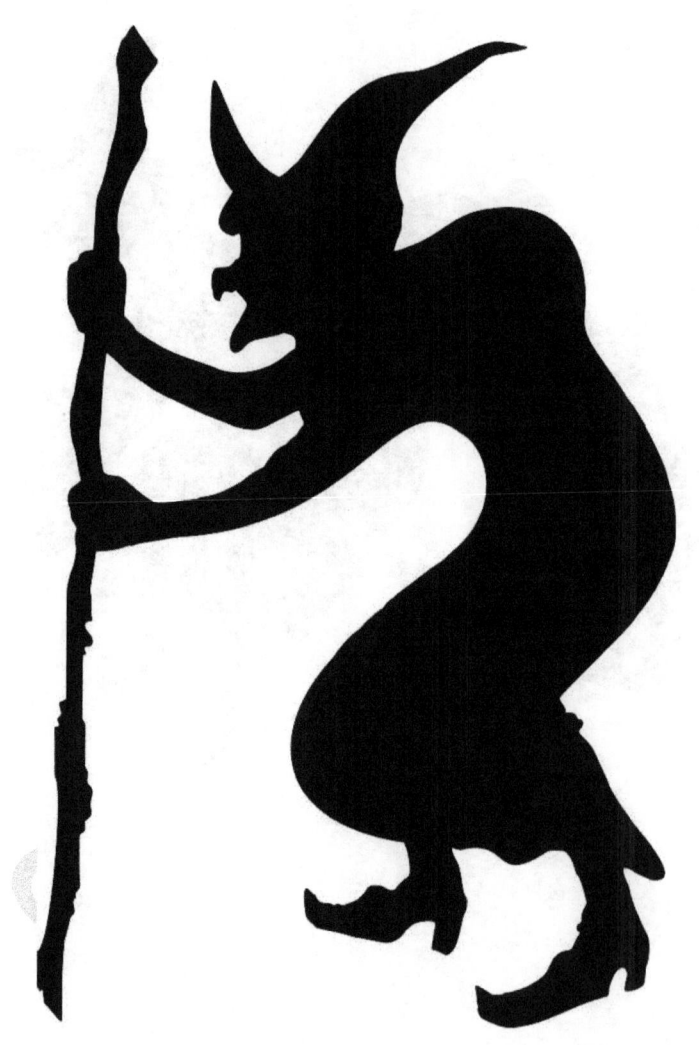

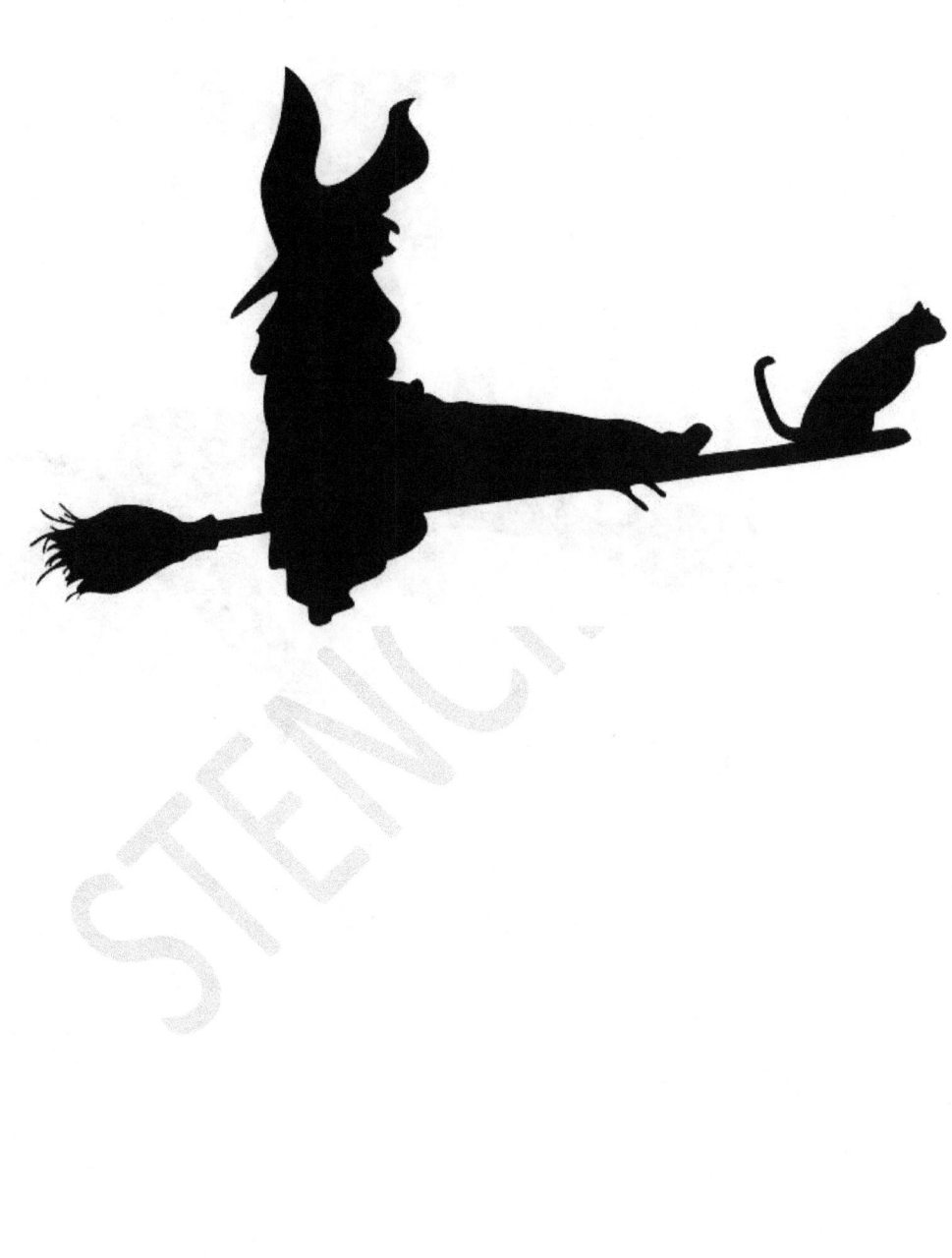
STENCIL

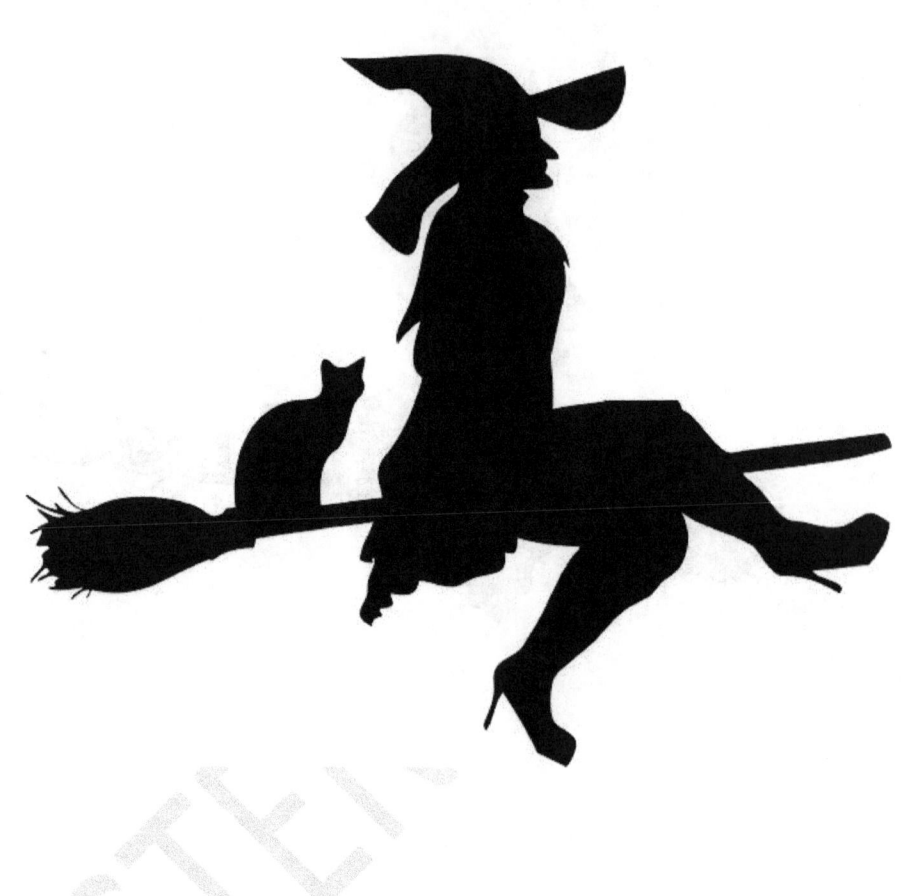

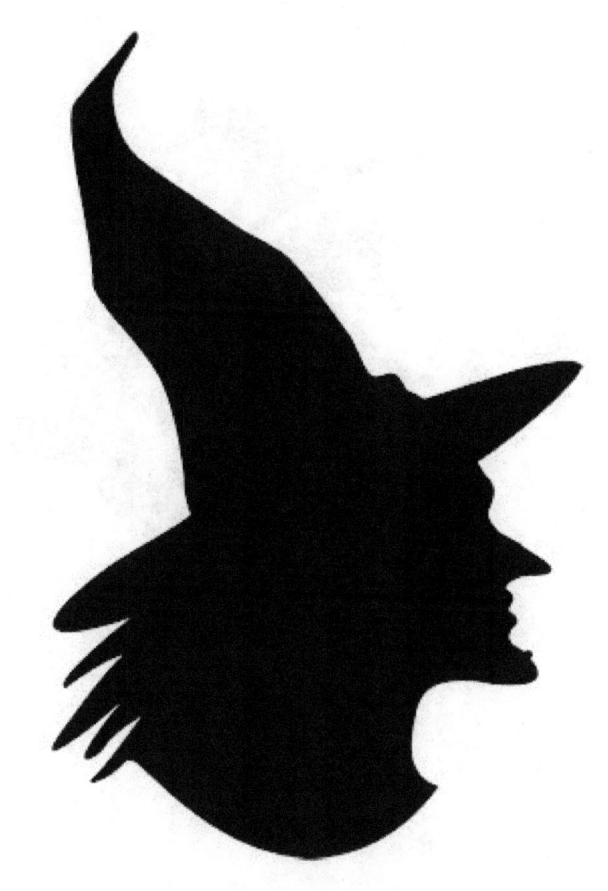

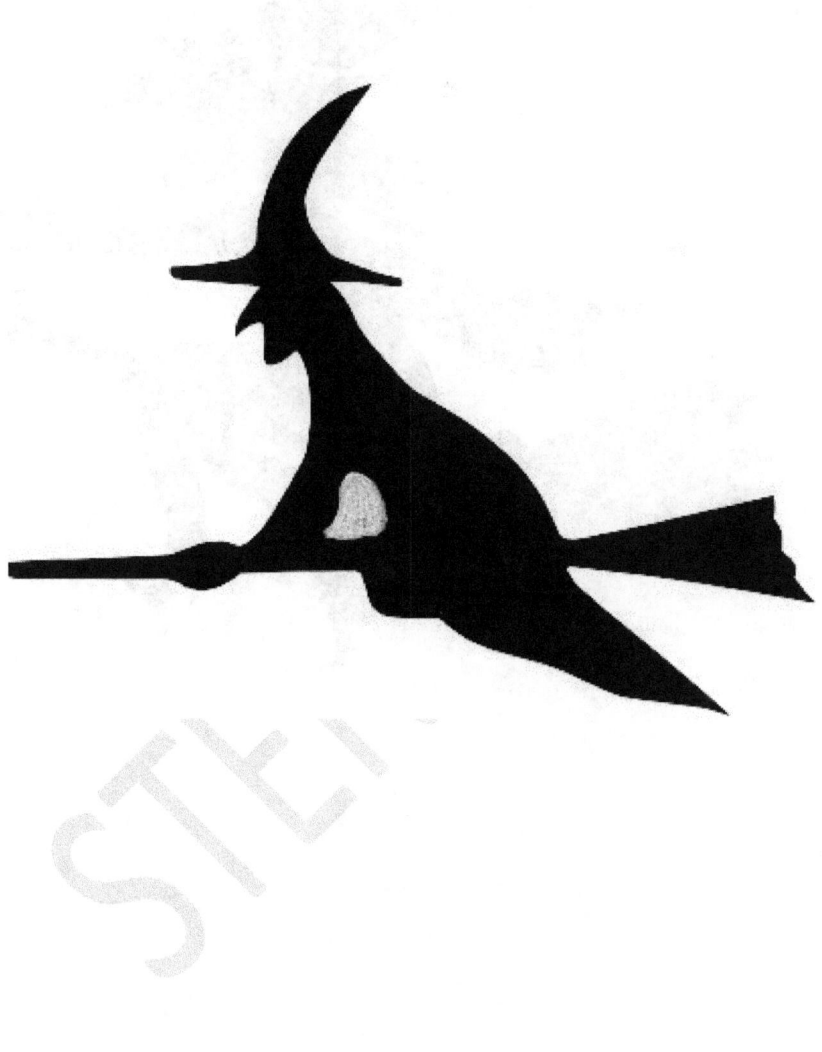

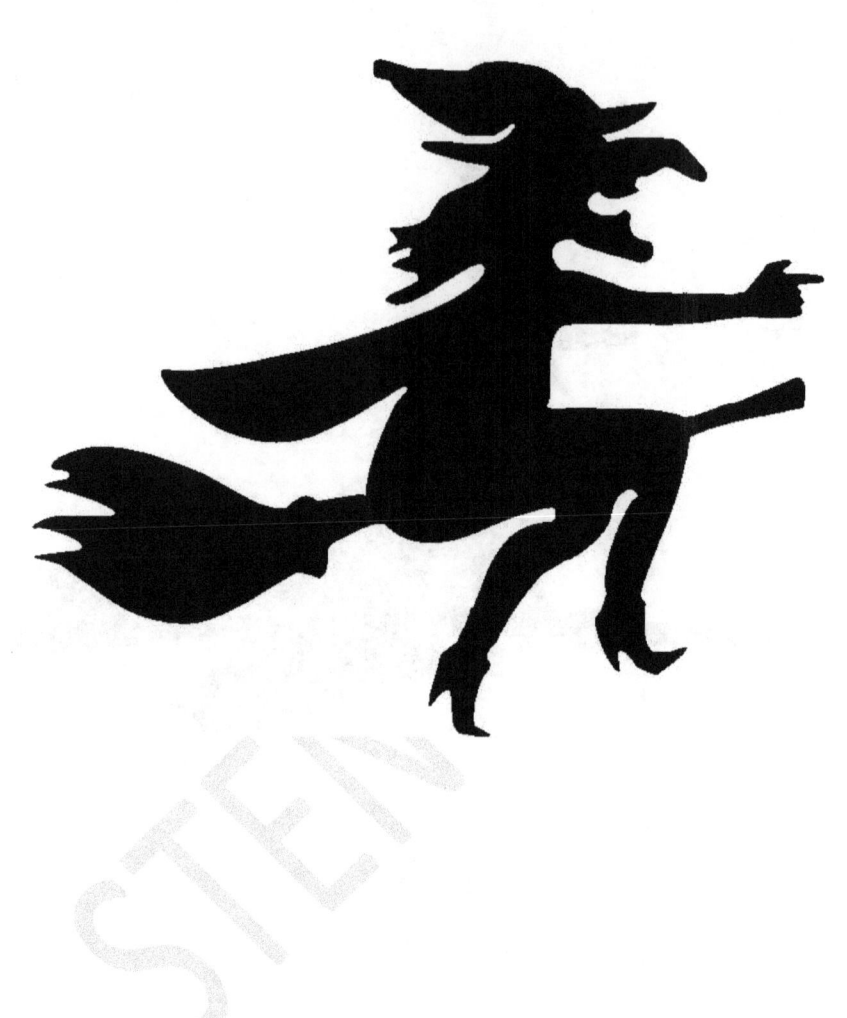
STEN

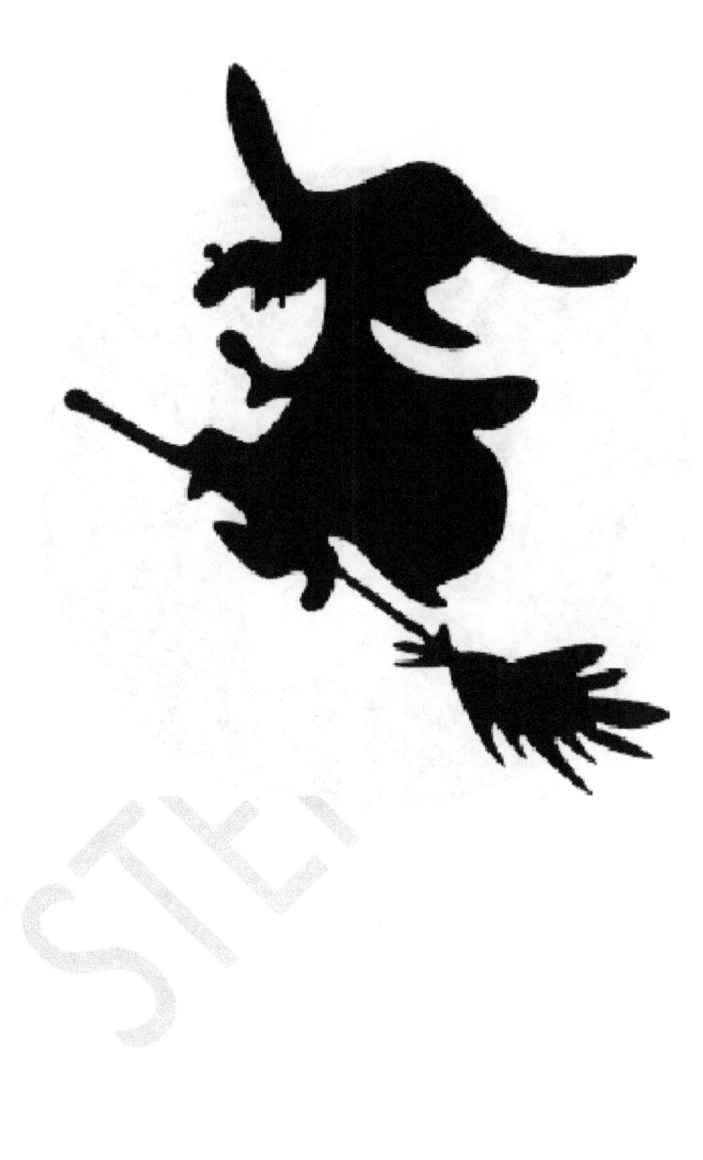
STE

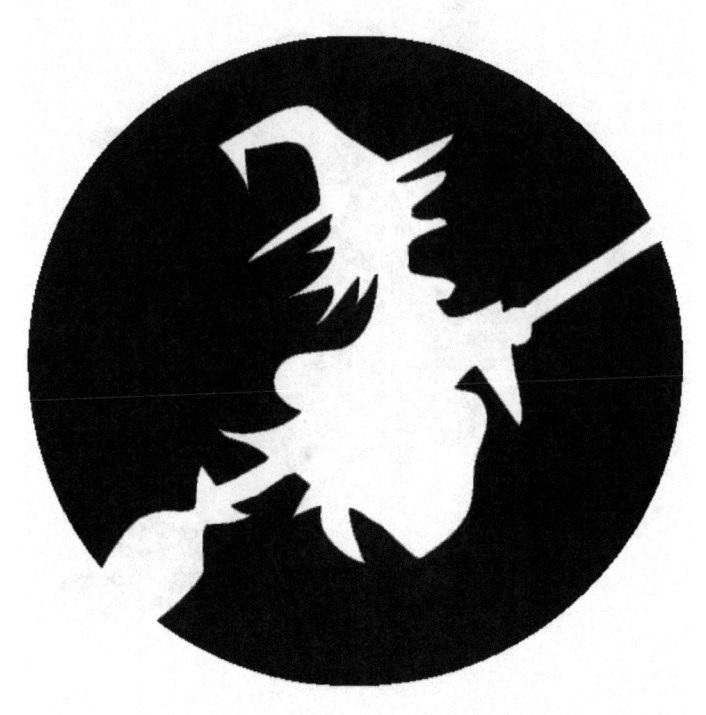

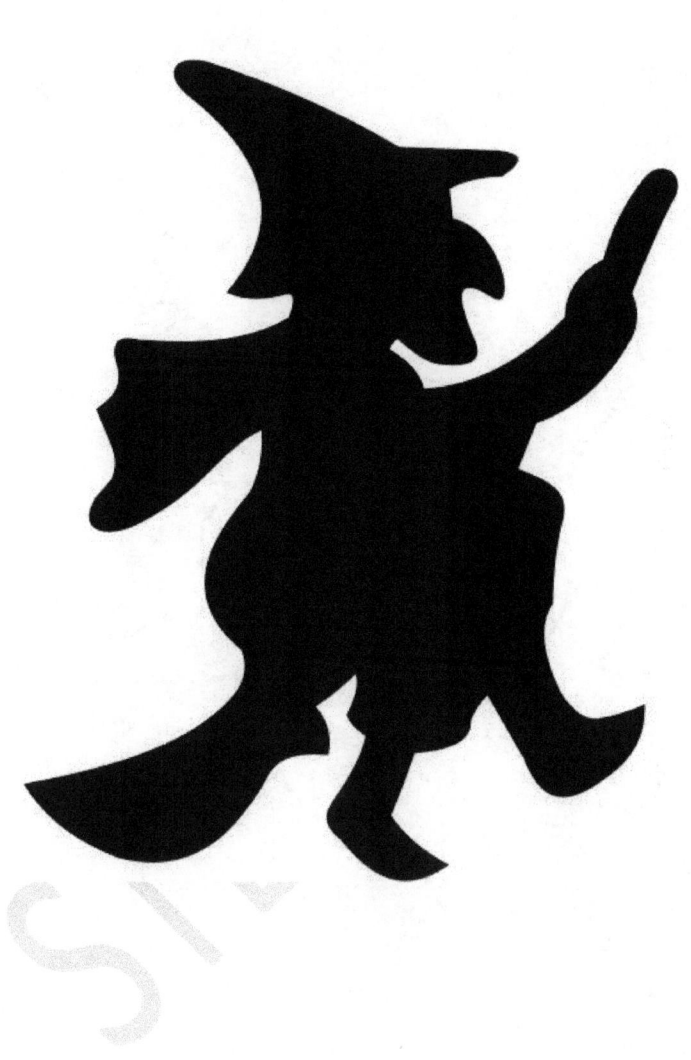

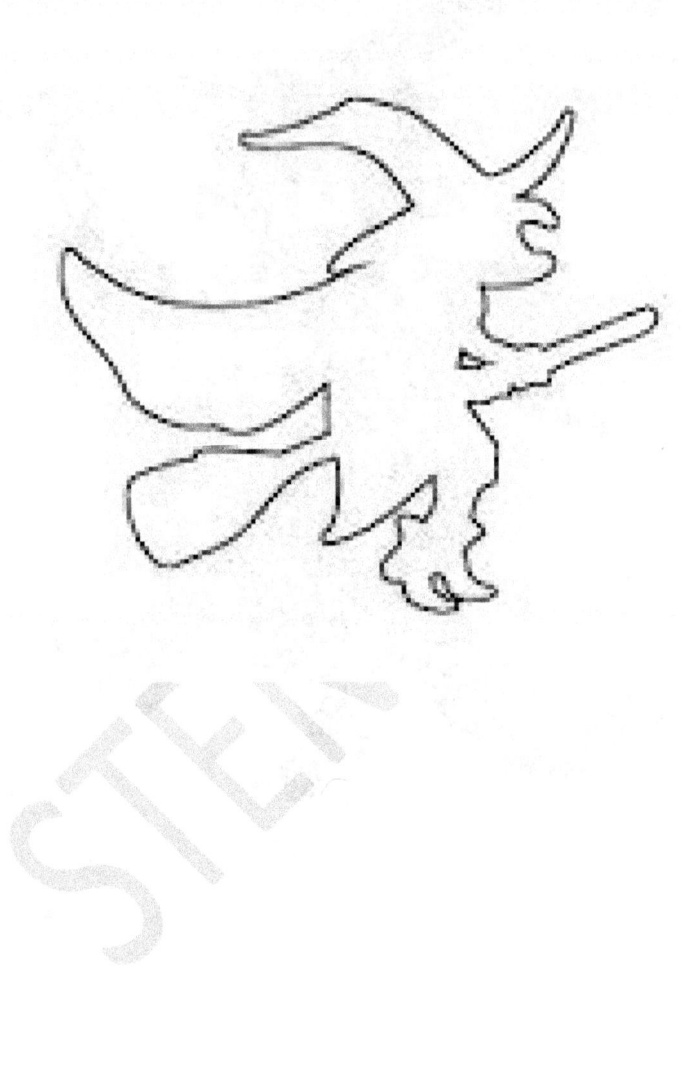

End of the book.

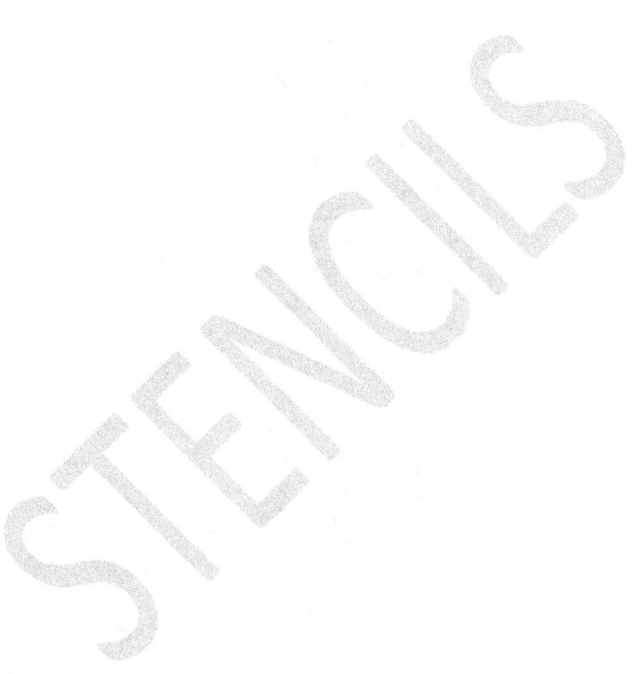

www.ingramcontent.com/pod-product-compliance
Lightning Source LLC
Chambersburg PA
CBHW071604170526
45166CB00004B/1792